Images
of
Oregon

First Printing October, 1991
Robert D. Shangle, Publisher

Library of Congress Cataloging-in-Publication Data
Images of Oregon
p.   cm.   ISBN 1-55988-303-0 (soft bound): $6.95
1. Oregon — Description and travel — 1981 — Views. I. LTA Publishing Company.
F877.I43 1991   917.9504'43 — dc20   91-22806 CIP

Copyright © 1991 by LTA Publishing Company
Production, Concept and Distribution by LTA Publishing Company, Portland, Oregon.
Printed in Thailand. This book produced as the major component of the "World Peace and
Understanding" program of Beauty of America Printing Company, Portland, Oregon.

Introduction

"What a beautiful area!" "I want to remember this forever!" "It's absolutely awesome!" "The Creator simply out-did Himself!"

All of these statements are descriptive of the thoughts expressed when viewing this great state of Oregon that we live in, work in, and play in. And why not. This is a Grand Place.

Images linger in our mind's eye, bringing back those memories of excitement, happiness, family, loved ones, places we've visited, or always dreamed of visiting. One can remember, either because "I've been there," or visited vicariously. We want to hold onto those experiences of "places I've been, things I've done, places I want to see."

The images in this book have been gathered together to assist with those memories and you can give it life. Combining these pictures with your memories make them fill with energy, telling your story that is full of excitement and thrills.

A tribute to Oregon!

Heceta Head Lighthouse

Crater Lake

Silver Falls State Park

Succor Creek, North of Jordan Valley

Japanese Gardens, Portland

Looking South from Neahkanie Mountain

Astoria Column

Multnomah Falls

Mount Hood and Lost Lake

Southern Oregon Coast near Cape Sebastian

Wallowa Lake

Deep Creek, East of Lakeview

Smith Rocks State Park

McKenzie Lava Beds

Broken Top Mountain

Cape Blanco, North of Port Orford

Battle Rock State Park

Elowah Falls, Columbia Gorge

Steens Mountain

Tumalo Falls

Columbia Gorge

Yaquina Lighthouse

Diamond Lake and Mt. Thielsen

Historic Jacksonville

Wallowa Mountains and Prairie Creek

The Painted Hills

Paulina Peak and Little Crater Lake

Portland

International Rose Test Gardens, Portland

State Capitol Building, Salem

Mt. Washington and Big Lake

Row River, South Willamette Valley

Sheep Rock, John Day Fossil Beds

Lone Ranch Beach Near Gold Beach

Sailing on the Columbia River

Fish Lake and Mount McLoughlin

Shitike Creek near Warm Springs

Mount Bachelor and Elk Lake

Upper Rogue River

North and Middle Sister Mountains from Scott Lake

Cape Meares

Fort Clatsop National Historic Site, near Astoria

Umpqua River

Willamette Valley from Mount Angel

Chetco River near Brookings

Mt. Jefferson

Sahalie Falls

Cannon Beach from Ecola State Park